THIS JOURNAL
FULLY BELONGS TO

_____

_____

ALL THE IMAGES
WERE CAPTURED DURING
MY TRAVELS TO STRANGE
AND BEAUTIFUL PLACES.

I THOUGHT I'D PUT THEM
INTO A "BORING POSTCARD"
BOOK SO YOU COULD PERHAPS
SHARE IT WITH THE WORLD.

OF COURSE WE ALL KNOW
THAT BEAUTY IS IN THE
EYE OF THE BEHOLDER.

IT'S A CREATIVE EXPERIMENT
AND MAYBE, JUST MAYBE
IT INSPIRES YOU.
EVEN A LITTLE IS COOL.

PEACE & LOVE,
MARTS

THIS PAGE IS FOR YOU
TO WRITE ANYTHING YOU WANT!

IO Oct 202I

Dear KEN,
I'm finally here in Japan
and all I can say is GLAD
I GOT a GUIDE! Everything
is so efficient & clean,
it makes Australia look
like an unwashed wet sock.
Too much to see - gotta
go, Peace and さようなら
Marts xxx

That Hurley dude

P.O. Box IIII

CASTLEMAINE,

Victoria, Australia

3450

PHOTOGRAPH BY MARTIN J HURLEY
YOGEEKNOTES.COM IMAGE CIRCA 2018

THE 'DIVIDED BACK' SIDE

#I A POSTCARD FROM OSAKA, JAPAN

IO Oct 2021

Dear James,
I thought you said BERLIN
would be EASY to navigate
if I had some basic German
down. No way man! I'm WAY
lost. My German just gets
me by! OH yeah, never seen
so many bicycles in one
place! Later dater,
Marts xxx

That Hurley dude

P.O. Box IIII

CASTLEMAINE,

Victoria, Australia

3450

PHOTOGRAPH BY MARTIN J HURLEY
YOGEEKNOTES.COM IMAGE CIRCA 2018

THE 'DIVIDED BACK' SIDE

#2 A POSTCARD FROM BERLIN, GERMANY

Dear Jules,
Melbourne has become a
student city. It's a
photographer's paradise
with hidden laneways and
classic buildings. Oh
yeah, someone had WAY TOO
much coffee today (ahem).
Blame it on all them
coffee shops.
Marts xxx

That Hurley dude

P.O. Box IIII

CASTLEMAINE,

Victoria, Australia

3450

THE 'DIVIDED BACK' SIDE

#3 A POSTCARD FROM MELBOURNE, AUSTRALIA

Dear Johnny Boy,
How could you not love
everything about New
Zealand? My guitar
brothers are here & they
always give me a Kiwi
welcome. Old school rules.
A land of opportunity
indeed. Kia ora.
Marts xxx

That Hurley dude

P.O. Box IIII

CASTLEMAINE,

Victoria, Australia

3450

PHOTOGRAPH BY MARTIN J HURLEY
YOGEEKNOTES.COM IMAGE CIRCA 2010

THE 'DIVIDED BACK' SIDE

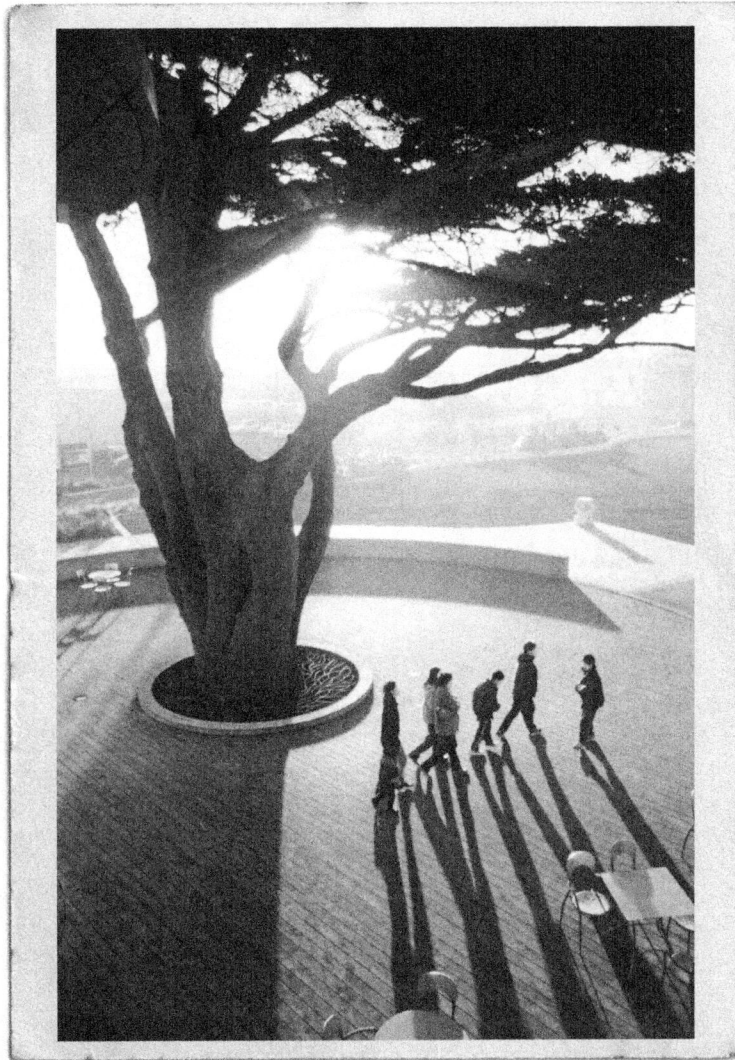

#4 A POSTCARD FROM WELLINGTON, NEW ZEALAND

10 Oct 2021

Dear Pumpkin,
Everything feels kinda
small in Japan. Like these
little cars parked in a
perfect position. You
gotta photograph this
stuff! It's unbelievable!
Marts xxx

That Hurley dude

P.O. Box IIII

CASTLEMAINE,

Victoria, Australia

3450

THE 'DIVIDED BACK' SIDE

#5 A POSTCARD FROM OSAKA, JAPAN

10 Oct 2021

Dear JS,
Here I am in India again.
They say confidence comes
from doing, so I spend a
lot of time doing. Some of
the things I've seen here
would BLOW your MIND!!
Enjoy the waves,
Marts xxx

That Hurley dude

P.O. Box IIII

CASTLEMAINE,

Victoria, Australia

3450

THE 'DIVIDED BACK' SIDE

#6 A POSTCARD FROM DARJEELING, INDIA

10 Oct 2021

Dear boss,
Did you know Brisbane was
a freakin' cool city? Bike
lanes everywhere. They
just gotta let me loose on
my e-scooter and the world
will be at peace.
Stay funky,
Marts xxx

That Hurley dude

P.O. Box IIII

CASTLEMAINE,

Victoria, Australia

3450

THE 'DIVIDED BACK' SIDE

#7 A POSTCARD FROM BRISBANE, AUSTRALIA

10 Oct 2021

Dear Jordo,
It's hard to wrap your
tongue around the name of
this city in Poland but I
love it. Apparently it
gets snowed in like crazy.
I managed to find one
coffee shop. Say no more.
Thanks for being you,
Marts xxx

That Hurley dude

P.O. Box IIII

CASTLEMAINE,

Victoria, Australia

3450

THE 'DIVIDED BACK' SIDE

#8 A POSTCARD FROM SZCZECIN, POLAND

10 Oct 2021

Dear Kevin,
Found myself well & truly
lost in Kolkata again. So
I snapped this for you.
Big ol' wide streets and a
gazillion years of
architectural history
here. This country is even
more CRAZY than Japan!
Marts xxx

That Hurley dude

P.O. Box IIII

CASTLEMAINE,

Victoria, Australia

3450

THE 'DIVIDED BACK' SIDE

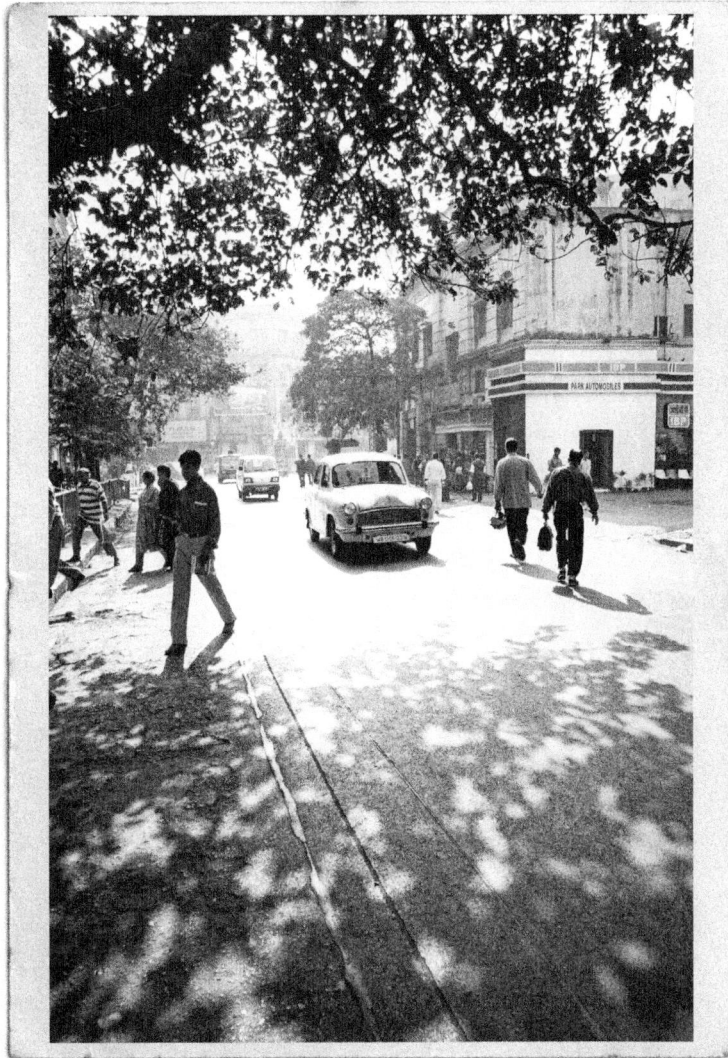

#9 A POSTCARD FROM KOLKATA, INDIA

10 Oct 2021

Dear Akiyo,
Oh no! I'm back in Chiang
Mai again. I'm a bit
templed-out but it's all
in the name of fun, right?
When I'm not taking photos
I'm watching you! You're
mesmerising!
Marts xxx

That Hurley dude

P.O. Box IIII

CASTLEMAINE,

Victoria, Australia

3450

THE 'DIVIDED BACK' SIDE

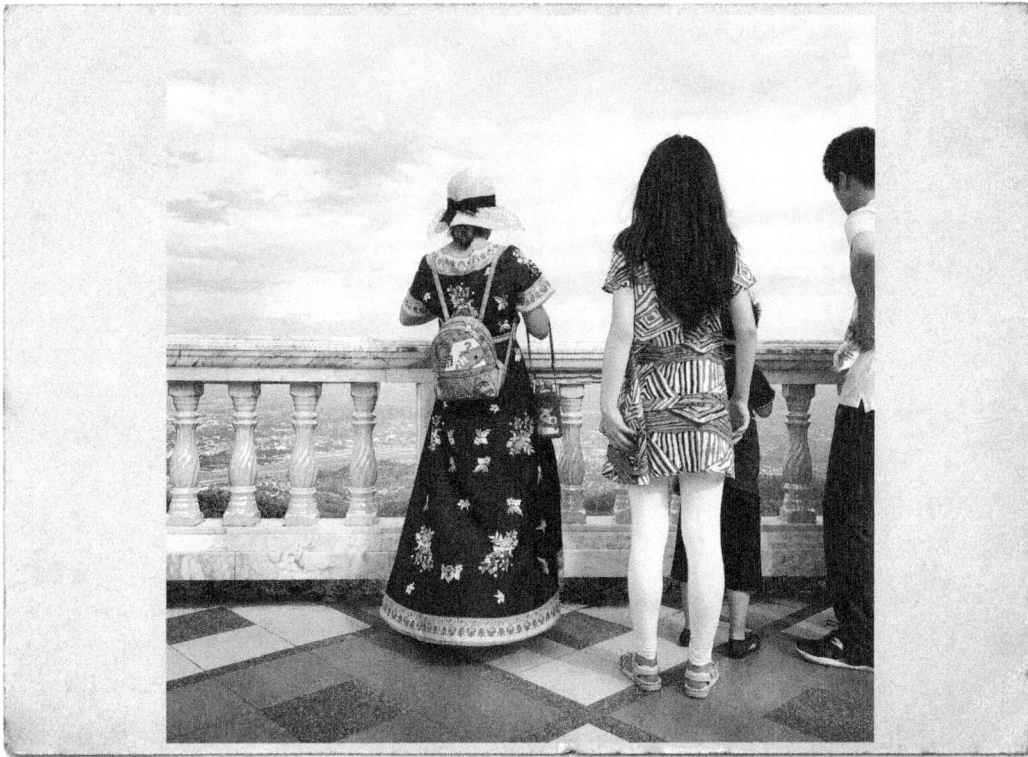

#10 A POSTCARD FROM CHIANG MAI, THAILAND

IO Oct 2021

BEST CHOICE · **BEST CHOICE**

INDIA POSTAGE · **PUTTALLA** · **STATES** · **ONE ANNA**

Dear Bob,
Here's a quick snap I took
while in Nagoya. Man I
LOVE this place! I got to
get off the peace pipe and
get more snaps happening.
PS. I saw a city called
Toyota too. Unreal.
Marts xxx

That Hurley dude

P.O. Box IIII

CASTLEMAINE,

Victoria, Australia

3450

PHOTOGRAPH BY MARTIN J HURLEY
YOGEEKNOTES.COM IMAGE CIRCA 2018

THE 'DIVIDED BACK' SIDE

#II A POSTCARD FROM NAGOYA, JAPAN

10 Oct 2021

Dear Peanut,
Sometimes I take photos
that I think are the BEST
thing EVER. Got to get
more people to SEE them.
Hence this book.
PS. Unreal.
Marts xxx

That Hurley dude

P.O. Box IIII

CASTLEMAINE,

Victoria, Australia

3450

PHOTOGRAPH BY MARTIN J HURLEY
YOGEEKNOTES.COM IMAGE CIRCA 2005

THE 'DIVIDED BACK' SIDE

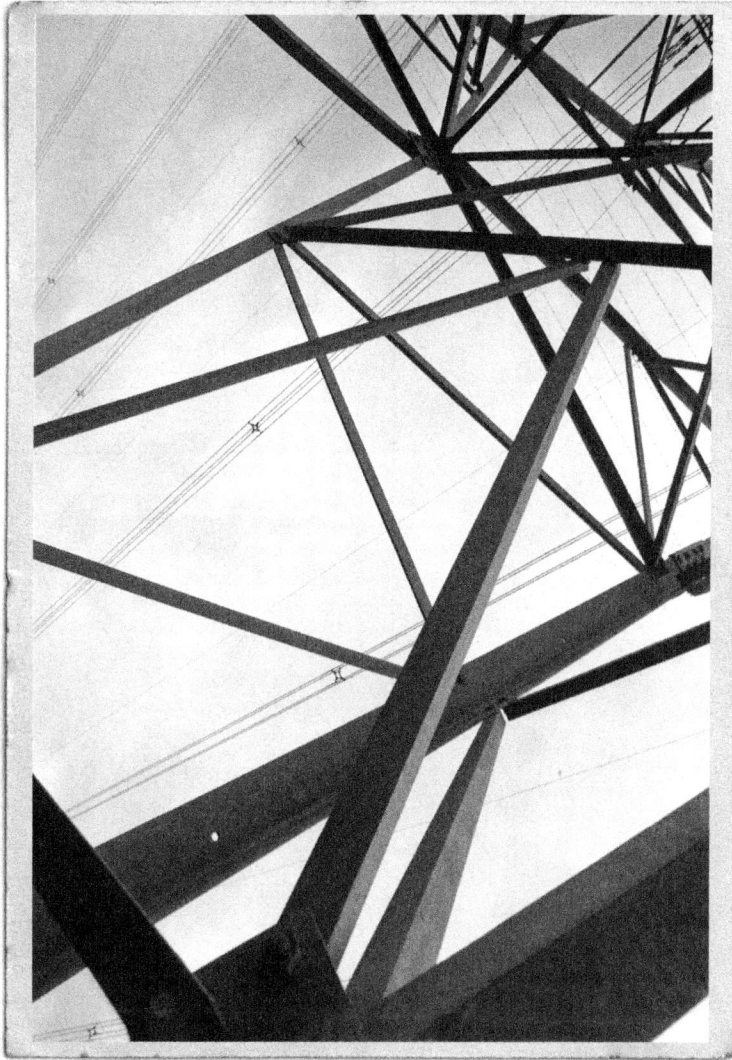

#12 A POSTCARD FROM VICTORIA, AUSTRALIA

IO Oct 202I

Dear J,
I forgot to get off the
Shinkansen and ended up in
Kagoshima. It's like
you're in another world.
My photos don't quite
catch what I need to say.
PS. Coffee is like 85 YEN
here. OH NO!
Marts xxx

That Hurley dude

P.O. Box IIII

CASTLEMAINE,

Victoria, Australia

3450

THE 'DIVIDED BACK' SIDE

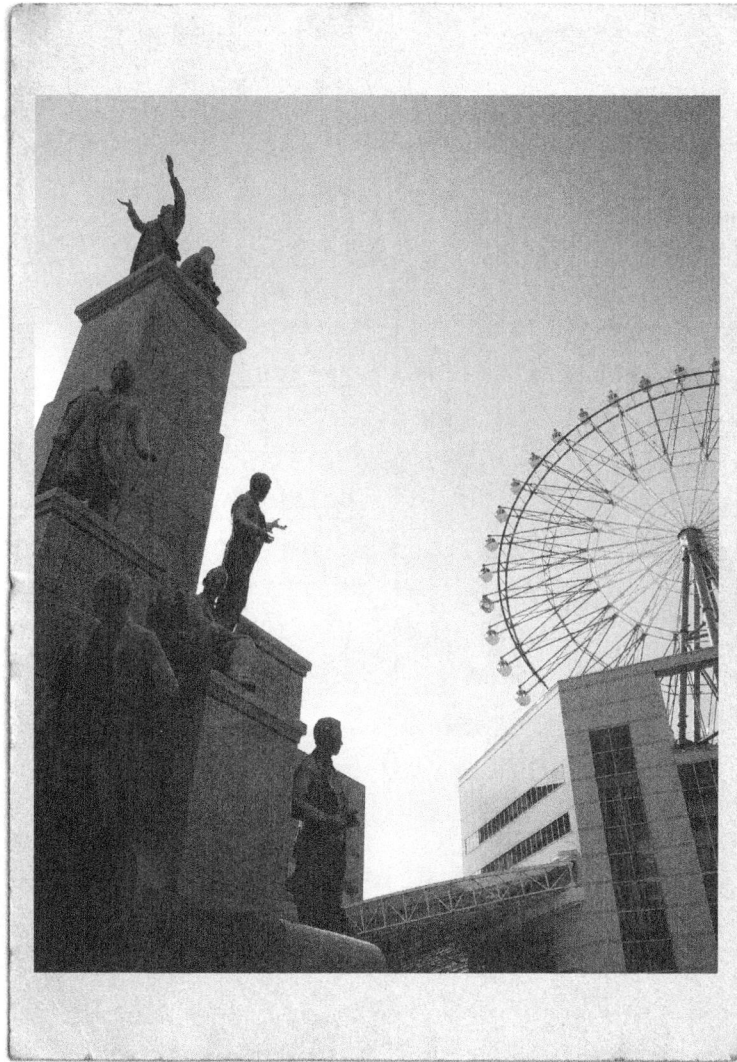

#13 A POSTCARD FROM KAGOSHIMA, JAPAN

10 Oct 2021

10 Oct 2021

Dear Si,
I called this cat "The
Running Man" and I'm still
not sure it works. But art
is a process of discovery,
right?
PS. Can't wait to see you
hangin' in Australia!
Marts xxx

That Hurley dude

P.O. Box IIII

CASTLEMAINE,

Victoria, Australia

3450

PHOTOGRAPH BY MARTIN J HURLEY
YOGEEKNOTES.COM IMAGE CIRCA 2015

THE 'DIVIDED BACK' SIDE

#14 A POSTCARD FROM BANGKOK, THAILAND

IO Oct 202I

Dear G,
This one is titled
'Stairway to Nowhere' or
something like that. I
thought I was the king of
the world when I took it!
Guess I still am!
Always nice hangin' with
you homie.
Marts xxx

That Hurley dude

P.O. Box IIII

CASTLEMAINE,

Victoria, Australia

3450

PHOTOGRAPH BY MARTIN J HURLEY
YOGEEKNOTES.COM IMAGE CIRCA 2002

THE 'DIVIDED BACK' SIDE

#I5 A POSTCARD FROM DELHI, INDIA

Dear David,
This one is titled 'Big
Ben and 5 Figures' & the
National Gallery of
Victoria (Aust) acquired
it. Hard to believe
sometimes! Guess I should
put my prices up!
Brings tears to the eyes.
Marts xxx

That Hurley dude

P.O. Box IIII

CASTLEMAINE,

Victoria, Australia

3450

THE 'DIVIDED BACK' SIDE

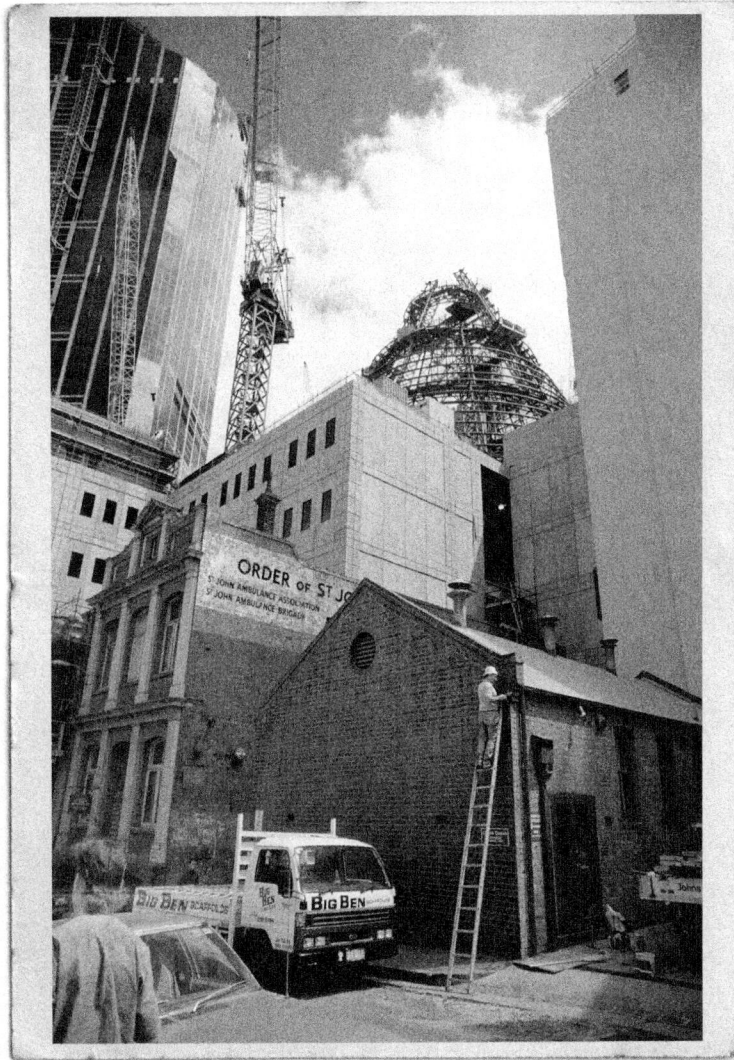

#16 A POSTCARD FROM MELBOURNE, AUSTRALIA

10 Oct 2021

INDIA POSTAGE STATE
PURIALA
ONE ANNA

Dear Miho,
I happened to be back in
KRABI Thailand and got
this snap when out on a
boat in the middle of the
ocean. The things I do to
get the shot. Sheesh!
PS. You're inspirational.
Marts xxx

That Hurley dude

P.O. Box IIII

CASTLEMAINE,

Victoria, Australia

3450

PHOTOGRAPH BY MARTIN J HURLEY
YOGEEKNOTES.COM IMAGE CIRCA 2019

THE 'DIVIDED BACK' SIDE

#17 A POSTCARD FROM KRABI, THAILAND

10 Oct 2021

INDIA POSTAGE
PU   ALL
STATE
ONE ANNA

Dear Paddy,
Stuck my beak into a
barber shop & produced
this shot. You could
almost call it perfect.
I'm bias of course but
hey.
PS. Love yr work. Unreal.
Marts xxx

That Hurley dude

P.O. Box IIII

CASTLEMAINE,

Victoria, Australia

3450

PHOTOGRAPH BY MARTIN J HURLEY
YOGEEKNOTES.COM IMAGE CIRCA 2015

THE 'DIVIDED BACK' SIDE

#18 A POSTCARD FROM KUALA LUMPUR, MALAYSIA

IO Oct 2021

BEST CHOICE ★ BEST CHOICE

INDIA POSTAGE
PUTTIALLA STATE
ONE ANNA

Dear Elon,
This little ditty is like
a side of a skyscraper.
Kinda magical. Like those
vehicles you make.
Buildings look tiny on
this postcard. Rock on.
Marts xxx

That Hurley dude

P.O. Box IIII

CASTLEMAINE,

Victoria, Australia

3450

PHOTOGRAPH BY MARTIN J HURLEY
YOGEEKNOTES.COM IMAGE CIRCA 2017

THE 'DIVIDED BACK' SIDE

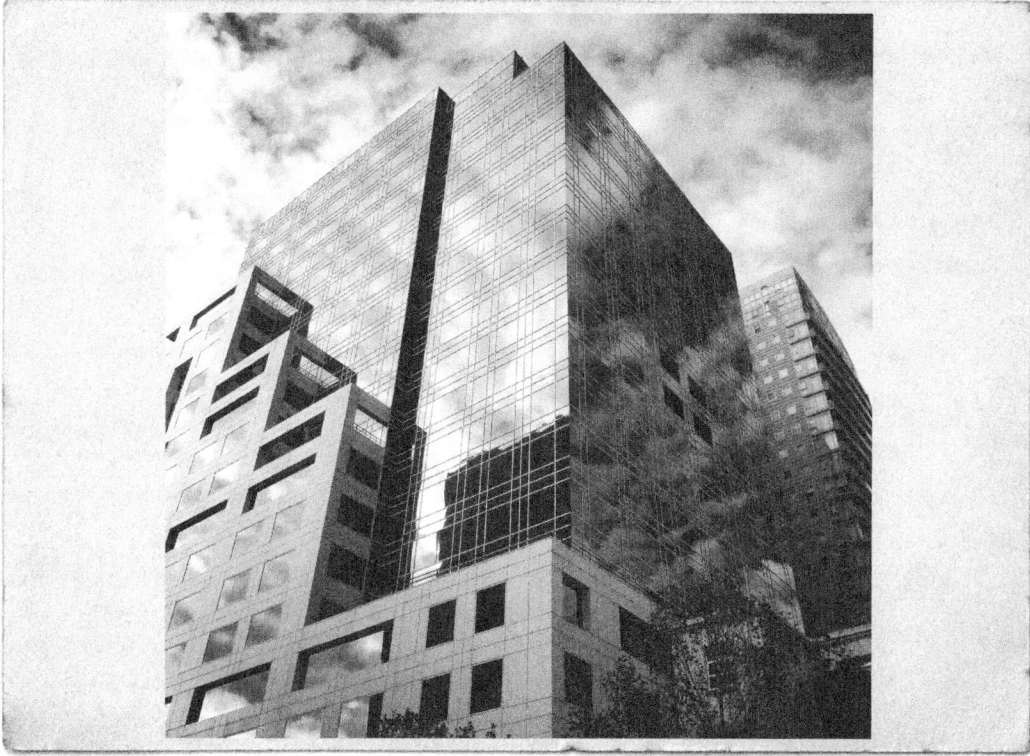

#19 A POSTCARD FROM MELBOURNE, AUSTRALIA

Dear Ringo,
When I'm in my photo-zone
it's like I'm in a bubble
of bliss. You just get to
dip into it sometimes.
Love this shot. SURREAL.
PS. Peace & Love brother.
Marts xxx

That Hurley dude

P.O. Box IIII

CASTLEMAINE,

Victoria, Australia

3450

PHOTOGRAPH BY MARTIN J HURLEY
YOGEEKNOTES.COM IMAGE CIRCA 2015

THE 'DIVIDED BACK' SIDE

#20 A POSTCARD FROM BANGKOK, THAILAND

10 Oct 2021

Dear Deano,
Back in Japan again and
everything is going NUTS.
Can't wait to bring you
here. It'd be hilarious!
Can you see the Jeffrey
Smart guy having a cig?
On yer bike!
Marts xxx

That Hurley dude

P.O. Box IIII

CASTLEMAINE,

Victoria, Australia

3450

PHOTOGRAPH BY MARTIN J HURLEY
YOGEEKNOTES.COM IMAGE CIRCA 2015

THE 'DIVIDED BACK' SIDE

#2I A POSTCARD FROM OSAKA, JAPAN

10 Oct 2021

Dear Raja,
The two figures are
standing on a dinosaur, so
I had to snap it. Can you
see it? There's an eye in
there somewhere. I could
keep doing this stuff all
day!
Back to work!
Marts xxx

That Hurley dude

P.O. Box IIII

CASTLEMAINE,

Victoria, Australia

3450

PHOTOGRAPH BY MARTIN J HURLEY
YOGEEKNOTES.COM   IMAGE CIRCA 2015

THE 'DIVIDED BACK' SIDE

#22 A POSTCARD FROM RAYONG, THAILAND

BEST CHOICE · BEST CHOICE

IO Oct 2021

INDIA POSTAGE · ONE ANNA

Dear Amanda,
I'm lost in another
Japanese subway again. But
I'm OK with that. Great
things happen sometimes,
out of the blue.
PS. Kyoto ROCKS.
Peace n love,
Marts xxx

That Hurley dude

P.O. Box IIII

CASTLEMAINE,

Victoria, Australia

3450

PHOTOGRAPH BY MARTIN J HURLEY
YOGEEKNOTES.COM IMAGE CIRCA 2015

THE 'DIVIDED BACK' SIDE

#23 A POSTCARD FROM KYOTO, JAPAN

10 Oct 2021

Dear Yogi,
It's weird but I really
related to this guy with
the pistolas. He was in
another world. I guess I'm
just fascinated how the
mind works.
PS. Guns weren't real but
the experience was.
Marts xxx

That Hurley dude

P.O. Box IIII

CASTLEMAINE,

Victoria, Australia

3450

PHOTOGRAPH BY MARTIN J HURLEY
YOGEEKNOTES.COM IMAGE CIRCA 2010

THE 'DIVIDED BACK' SIDE

#24 A POSTCARD FROM TRANG, THAILAND

Dear Dr,
I need help. I'm always
taking photos of things
like buildings and people
at work. Like these cats
doing some Thai style
construction. Unreal man!
Now, where was I?
Marts xxx

That Hurley dude

P.O. Box IIII

CASTLEMAINE,

Victoria, Australia

3450

THE 'DIVIDED BACK' SIDE

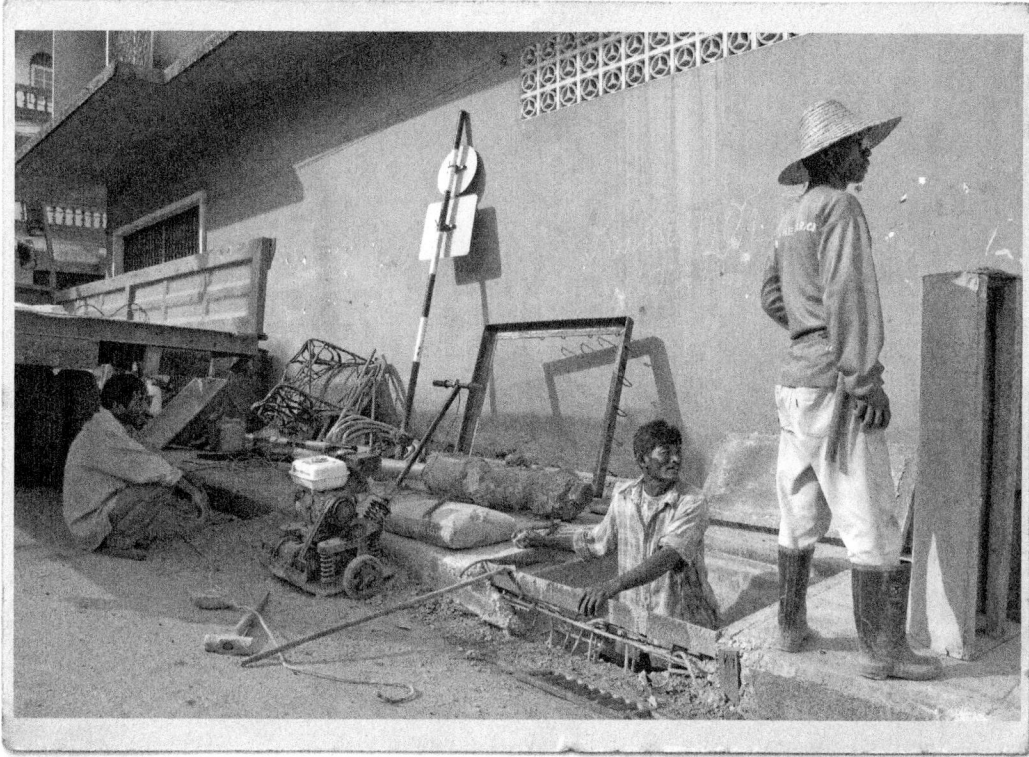

#25 A POSTCARD FROM TRANG, THAILAND

10 Oct 2021

Dear Fandaego,
Here is a picture of a
water tower somewhere in
India. I think there is a
bird in it too. Man, I
really got to get off the
chocolate before I go MAD.
PS. I got your back,
Marts xxx

That Hurley dude

P.O. Box IIII

CASTLEMAINE,

Victoria, Australia

3450

PHOTOGRAPH BY MARTIN J HURLEY
YOGEEKNOTES.COM IMAGE CIRCA 2002

THE 'DIVIDED BACK' SIDE

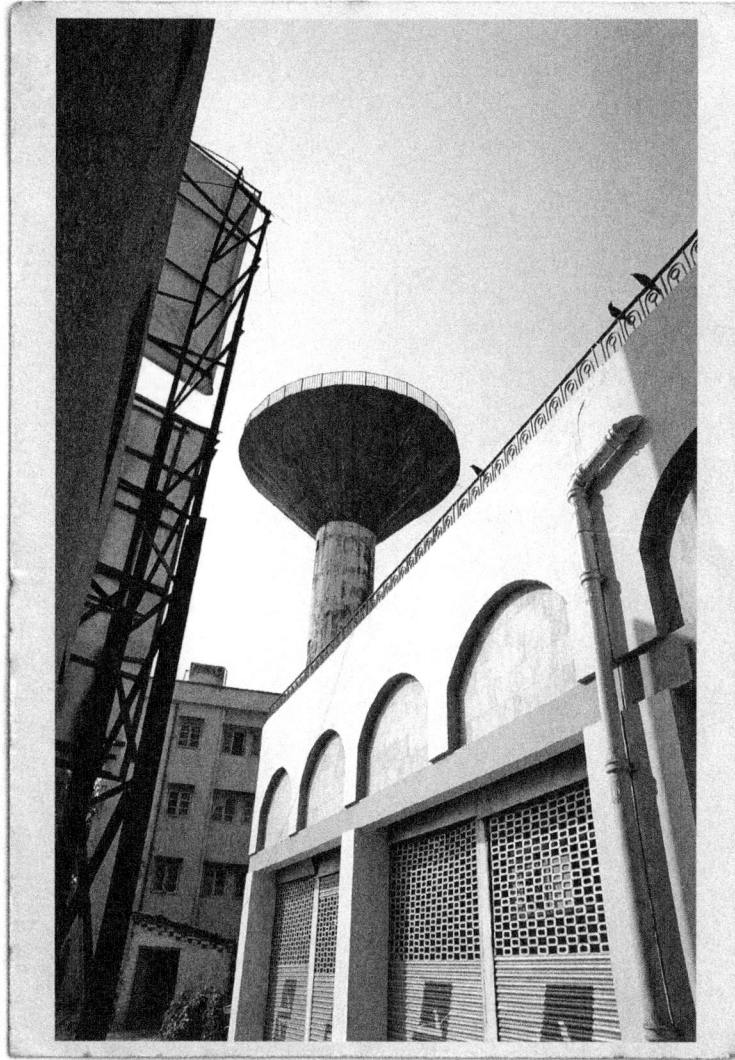

#26 A POSTCARD FROM SOMEWHERE, INDIA

Dear TG,
There I go again, taking
random photos of people
living a normal life. Why
can't I be normal too?
Hold on, who wants to be
normal?
PS. Some moments are
really precious.
Marts xxx

That Hurley dude

P.O. Box IIII

CASTLEMAINE,

Victoria, Australia

3450

THE 'DIVIDED BACK' SIDE

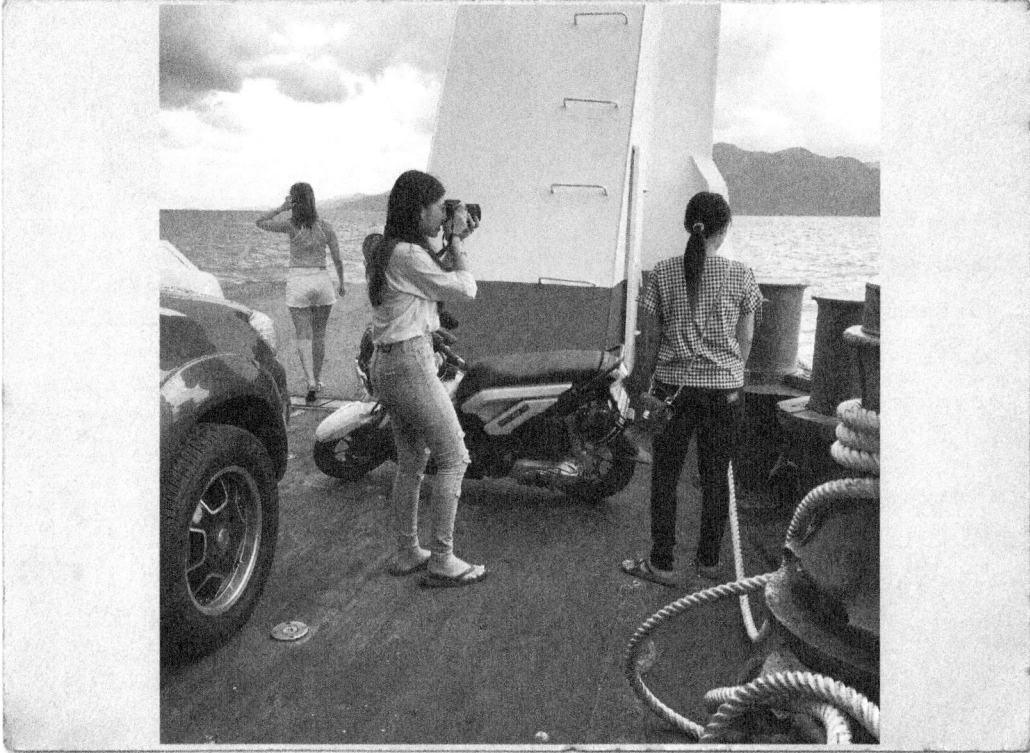

#27 A POSTCARD FROM THE OCEAN, THAILAND

IO Oct 202I

Dear P,
This cat was too cool not
to be caught in a Hurley
moment. I got to say, I
love how creatively free I
feel in Japan, pretty much
everywhere I go.
PS. Life is groovy eh?
Marts xxx

That Hurley dude

P.O. Box IIII

CASTLEMAINE,

Victoria, Australia

3450

THE 'DIVIDED BACK' SIDE

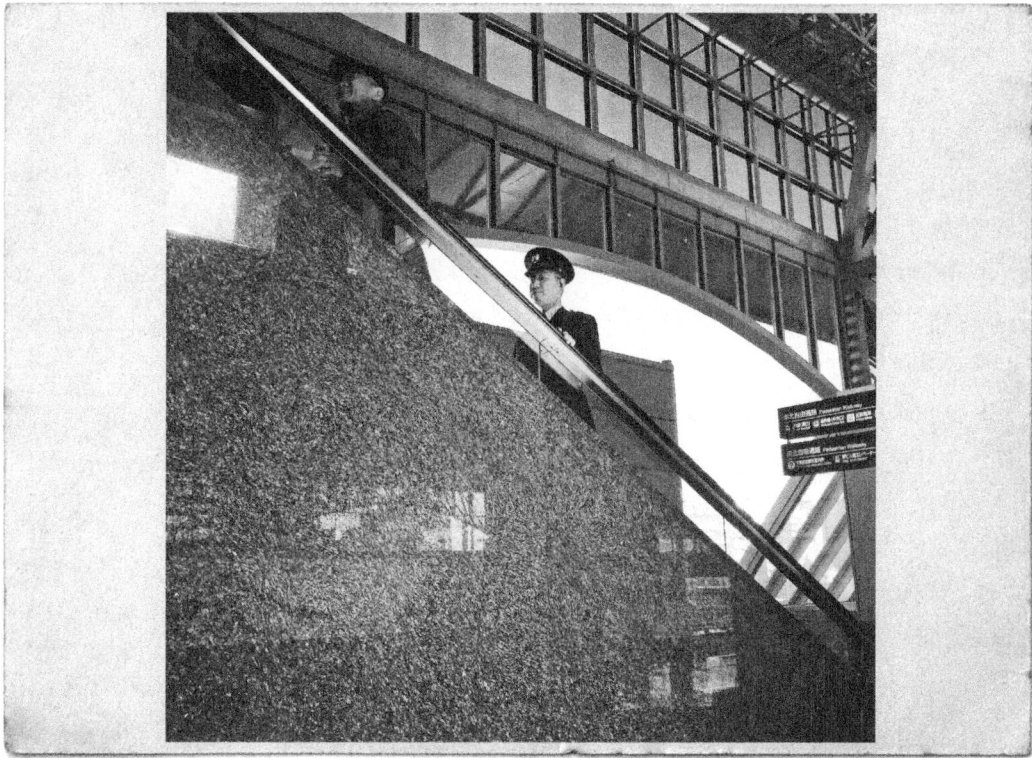

#28 A POSTCARD FROM KYOTO, JAPAN

IO Oct 202I

Dear G,
This snap kinda didn't
make the Hurley TOP IO but
it snuck in here somehow.
So yeah, just touching
base. I gotta say I love
how you live LIFE to the
fullest. Inspirational!
PS. Unreal!
Marts xxx

That Hurley dude

P.O. Box IIII

CASTLEMAINE,

Victoria, Australia

3450

PHOTOGRAPH BY MARTIN J HURLEY
YOGEEKNOTES.COM IMAGE CIRCA 2015

THE 'DIVIDED BACK' SIDE

#29 A POSTCARD FROM BANGKOK, THAILAND

10 Oct 2021

Dear friend,
This is the last "boring
postcard" in the book! The
sky is going to fall in
now. Of course, I made
sure it was snapped in
Japan. I'm lost for words.
PS. Stay friendly to
animals.
Marts xxx

That Hurley dude

P.O. Box IIII

CASTLEMAINE,

Victoria, Australia

3450

THE 'DIVIDED BACK' SIDE

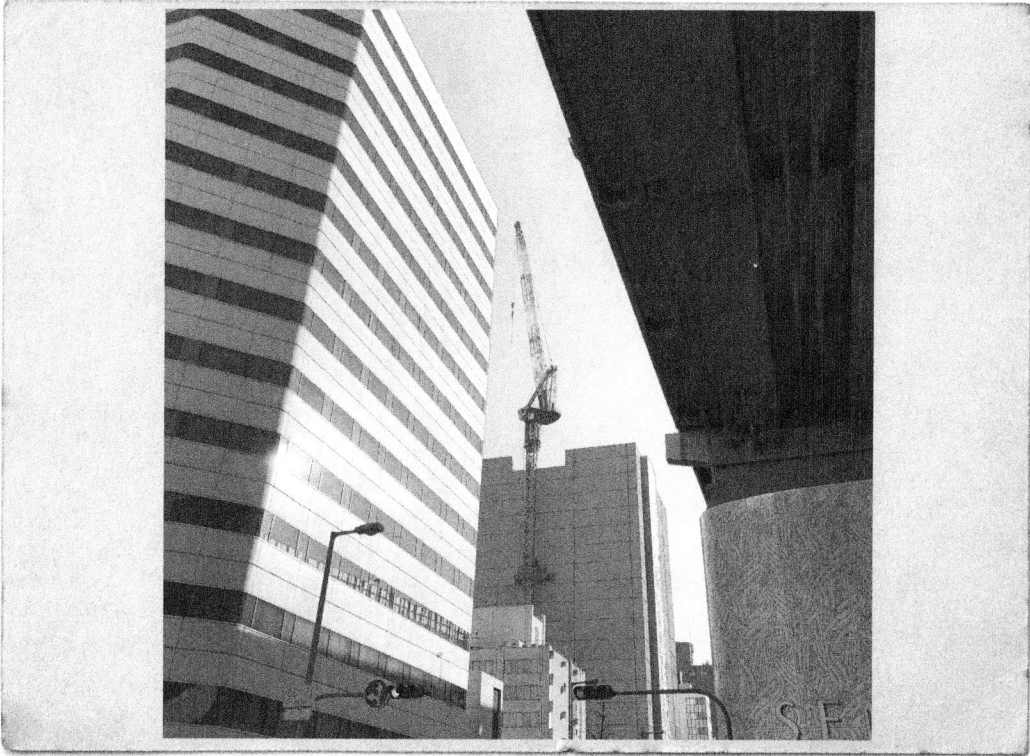

#30 A POSTCARD FROM OSAKA, JAPAN

THE KEY IS TO KEEP COMPANY
ONLY WITH PEOPLE WHO
UPLIFT YOU, WHOSE PRESENCE
CALLS FORTH YOUR BEST.

- EPICTETUS

Printed in Dunstable, United Kingdom